Some essays on golf-course architecture

H S Colt, C H Alison

fine
NP
65
C7

SOME ESSAYS ON GOLF-COURSE ARCHITECTURE

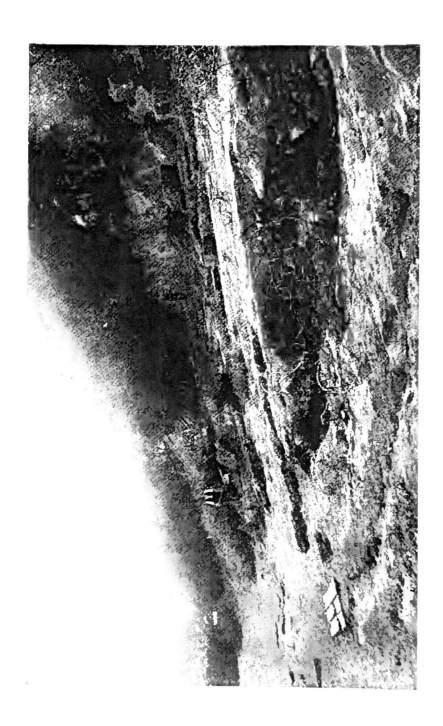

SOME ESSAYS ON GOLF-COURSE ARCHITECTURE

BY

H. S. COLT

AND

C. H. ALISON

WITH CONTRIBUTIONS BY

DR. A. MACKENZIE
HORACE G. HUTCHINSON
JOHN L. LOW, AND OTHERS

LONDON
PUBLISHED AT THE OFFICES OF "COUNTRY LIFE," 20,
TAVISTOCK STREET, COVENT GARDEN; W C.2, AND BY
GEORGE NEWNES, LTD., 8-11, SOUTHAMPTON STREET,
STRAND, W.C.2. NEW YORK: CHARLES SCRIBNER'S SONS
MCMXX

PREFACE

Iт is sometimes difficult to realise the present popularity
of the game of golf. No other game has been played so
universally, and it is quickly becoming a necessary recreation
for mankind throughout the world. To some readers this
may seem to be an exaggeration, but if the present position
is carefully considered, the statement will appear to be true.

I recently left the neighbourhood of Sunningdale, and as
I thought, of golf-courses, to live far away from any large
town, and in the midst of an intensely rural district. After
spending nearly twenty years in the closest connection with
the game, I thought that it would perhaps be a relief to
have my home far removed from the sight and sound of it,
so that it might be possible to emerge from home fresh and
keen for my work as a golf-course architect. But I very
soon realised on a fine Sunday afternoon that the joy of
life was not complete. There was a craving for my usual
game round the Swinley Forest course, and then I made a
few inquiries, and to my surprise discovered, almost at my
door, a very delightful 9-hole course. When I came to
live in the neighbourhood I had never even heard of it, but
now I know that it is an impossibility in this country to get
away from the game, or for many to be deprived of it without
severely feeling the loss.

France is quickly adopting golf as her national game.
It is only a few years ago that it was unknown in that country
except at a few holiday resorts, and now we find that one
of the Paris clubs has a membership of over a thousand.
Spain is becoming enthusiastic, and at Madrid there is a
club with over 600 members.

The progress made in America is well known, but to me
it was a surprise in 1913, when I paid my second visit to
the United States, to hear that in the neighbourhood of
Chicago there were between thirty and forty courses.

But the world-wide popularity of the game was brought home to me at Sunningdale a few years ago when a large party of Japanese spent the Christmas holidays there, and showed very plainly that we should have to reckon seriously with competition from that country in future championship contests.

It is therefore unnecessary to offer an apology for a book on Golf-course Architecture. I have personally written on this subject in Mr. Martin Sutton's *Book of the Links*, but owing to the ever-increasing army of golfers, and also the novel conditions, which are constantly arising, under which the game is to be played, a book devoted entirely to the subject may be found useful. Moreover, golfers are becoming more and more interested in the architecture and construction of courses. They realise that there is no other pursuit in the open air which gives them the same relaxation from the worries of life. To some the healthy exercise, and the battle of the game played with a keen opponent, are the attractions; but to others the rest gained from a round played with a pleasant companion on a fine spring morning, on a course with beautiful natural surroundings, gives the greatest pleasure, and the actual result of such matches is not of paramount importance.

The landscape work on a course is therefore growing more important every day, as players become more conscious of the increased enjoyment derived from a delightful environment, in the same way that a beautiful setting enhances the beauty of the jewel.

An architect would have a poor chance of being the means of furthering this enjoyment unless the materials upon which he worked possessed variety. It is this constant variety which makes his work so fascinating. The conditions existing in the Riviera, for instance, are so utterly different from those, say, in the West of Ireland. The game must even be played on heavy flat clay fields, as well as on the short crisp turf near the sea-shore. I say advisedly "must," as otherwise there would be large districts without one of the greatest necessities of the age.

The interest of wrestling with the difficulties of unsuitable conditions is no doubt one of the many charms of this occupation. And after seeing some courses which have been made out of materials which, a few years ago, I should personally have refused to dedicate to the game, the observer is compelled to admit that, with skilful treatment and an adequate supply of money, relaxation and sport can be obtained for almost any locality, provided the land be not too mountainous.

Players are beginning to see how easy it is to place bunkers at correct distances, but few perhaps realise how difficult it is to arrange for the natural features to provide to the fullest possible extent the necessary excitement for the course, and to supplement these features without destroying the natural beauty of the site. When this has been accomplished, the necessary vitality will have been gained, without which the experienced architect will obtain no real satisfaction.

That is the real test of a course, Is it going to live?—not, Does it provide a test for the game? There is more than that necessary. The bunkers may be placed correctly, the putting-greens may be true, the lies perfect, and yet no really satisfying enjoyment will be obtained by the critical and experienced player.

There can be no true and lasting success for such a creation, and it will die in the course of years. An architect's earnest hope is, without doubt, that his courses will have the necessary vitality to resist possibly adverse criticism, and will endure as a lasting record of his craft and of his love for his work.

We wish to acknowledge the receipt of many photographs of courses and interesting letters relating to the progress of the game in various parts of the world. It has been impossible to include in this book everything which has been received, but we desire to thank all our correspondents for the kindly interest which they have shown.

H. S. COLT.

CONTENTS

CHAPTER I

GOLF IN THE NINETIES

Suburban golf—Victorian construction—Early seaside golf—Has progress been universal?—Questions   .   .   .   . pp. 13–18

CHAPTER II

THE MODERN COURSE—FRAMEWORK

Two starting-points—Sites for putting-greens—The blind approach—Length—Length of individual holes—Range of teeing-grounds—General   .   .   .   . pp. 19–26

CHAPTER III

THE PLACING OF BUNKERS

Compulsory carries from the tee—Optional carries—Compulsory carries for the second shot—Other bunkers—Short holes—Protective hazards   .   .   .   . pp. 27-39

CHAPTER IV

CONSTRUCTION

The golfing point of view—Putting-greens—Gradients—Freak greens—The entrance to the green—The nature of the hazards—Artificial sand-bunkers—Landscape—What to avoid—An open view—Artificial hazards—Nature the model—Economy   .   . pp. 40-52

CHAPTER V

FINANCIAL CONSIDERATIONS

Demand and supply—Accessibility—The quality of the golf—Other attractions—Conclusion . . . . . . pp. 53–56

CHAPTER VI

LABOUR-SAVING MACHINERY AND THE COST OF CONSTRUCTION

Mole-drainage machine: comparative cost of mole drainage—The turf-cutting machine : comparative cost—The scraper or scoop : comparative cost—General . . . . pp. 57–61

CHAPTER VII

GOLF IN BELGIUM . . . . . . pp. 62–64

CHAPTER VIII

OTHER OPINIONS . . . . . . pp. 65–69

ILLUSTRATIONS

GRANGE-OVER-SANDS . . . . *Frontispiece*

FACING PAGE

FIFTH GREEN AT MOORTOWN, NEAR LEEDS . . 18

EDEN GOLF-COURSE, ST. ANDREWS 19

LONGNIDDRY DURING CONSTRUCTION . . . 36

LONGNIDDRY DURING CONSTRUCTION . . . 37

PINE VALLEY, PHILADELPHIA : FIFTH HOLE . . 40

PINE VALLEY, PHILADELPHIA : TENTH HOLE . . 41

PINE VALLEY, PHILADELPHIA : THE SITE FOR THE
    FIFTEENTH TEE 42

PINE VALLEY, PHILADELPHIA : EIGHTEENTH TEE . 43

MADRID : THE FOURTH HOLE 48

ROSAPENNA LINKS, CO. DONEGAL 49

ST. GEORGE'S HILL, WEYBRIDGE 50

SUNNINGDALE : THE EIGHTH GREEN 51

TURF-CUTTING MACHINE AT WORK 58

THE SCRAPER CONVERTING THE FLAT INTO UNDULATING
    LAND 59

GROUP TAKEN AT THE ST. CLOUD COUNTRY CLUB, PARIS 62

KNOCKE : SECOND GREEN ON BIG COURSE . . 63

HAMILTON, ONTARIO : THE ELEVENTH TEE . . 66

TORONTO GOLF-COURSE, CANADA 67

SOME ESSAYS ON GOLF-COURSE ARCHITECTURE

CHAPTER I

GOLF IN THE NINETIES

By C. H. ALISON

WHEN the game of Golf began to achieve its widespread popularity in England, a demand naturally arose for golf-courses in the immediate neighbourhood of the large towns. Prior to 1890 the game had been played, for the most part, either on seaside links or on common land. But the new generation of golfers, many of whom were busy men, were unwilling or unable to waste precious time in travelling, and therefore tackled the problem of creating golf-courses on any land which was available in the suburbs.

SUBURBAN GOLF

The soil with which they had to deal was in many cases very heavy. Agricultural drainage usually existed, but this, although sufficient to prevent cattle from getting trench feet, was by no means effective in securing firm lies and stances for the golfer. Through the winter months the ball frequently stuck where it pitched, and was almost invariably covered with mud. As regards the putting-greens, the green-keeper relied mainly on the heavy roller for obtaining an even surface. He had not yet discovered the art of creating a porous soil in which the fine grasses could flourish, and which would remain firm in wet weather. The use of sand, except on the teeing-grounds, was practically unknown, and no worm-killer had been invented. In winter the greens, therefore, were so soft that they were covered with heel-marks, while the worm-casts, flattened out by the roller, formed greasy patches of mud, which smothered the grasses underneath. The whole surface of the greens became hopelessly caked through over-rolling, and even in summer, when they were a trifle better, there were usually a large number of bare patches.

VICTORIAN CONSTRUCTION

The construction of these courses was simple in the extreme. There was only one form of bunker. This consisted of a rampart built of sods with a trench in front of it, filled with a sticky substance, usually dark red in colour. The face of the rampart was perpendicular. It was precisely 3 ft. 6 ins. in height throughout, and ran at an exact right-angle to the line of play. The number of these obstacles varied according to the length of the hole. A short hole required one, a drive and pitch required two, a long hole three. A stranger, therefore, was able to ascertain the bogey of any given hole by counting the number of bunkers, and adding two to this total. Conversely, if it appeared that the length of a hole justified making the bogey four, a simple subtraction sum informed the green committee that two bunkers were required.

There were no side-hazards except long grass and trees. The fairway was invariably rectangular, and the putting greens were square and flat. Some clubs could not afford to make all their putting-greens quite flat, but in such cases the host would apologise to his guest when an undulating green was reached.

It will be realised that this stereotyped placing of bunkers rendered the game extremely monotonous, and that, while the indifferent player was usually penalised for a topped shot, the good golfer seldom had a moment of excitement, and hardly ever got into trouble unless he played abnormally wide of the line. Moreover, the rampart style of bunker did not add to the beauty of the landscape, or lend an additional thrill to the stroke by its awe-inspiring appearance.

Another notable feature about suburban golf-course architecture in the nineties was the extreme flatness of the approaches. Any bold features which existed were used as hazards for the tee shot if they were used at all. Very seldom was a green placed in such a position as to render the approach play naturally interesting, while to create grass slopes or hollows artificially was an unknown art. Any golfer who has played the eleventh and twelfth holes on the old course at St. Andrews, the seventeenth hole on the old course at Walton Heath, or the third hole at Stoke Poges, will realise what a vast amount of interest is added to the approach play by the lie of the land in front of these greens. If the player has gauged his shot correctly and struck the ball truly he enjoys the intense pleasure of seeing it run firmly up to the hole ; while if his stroke is untruly struck he experiences the almost painful thrill of seeing it shouldered away from the green and perhaps sucked into an adjacent bunker. If these approaches lay over flat ground they would be robbed of almost all their interest, and it is therefore evident that the suburban golfer who did not encounter difficulties of this type missed a very striking feature in the game.

Early Seaside Golf

In sand-dune country some excellent courses already existed in 1890, but in constructing new courses near the sea there was in the Victorian Era a general tendency to take all hazards at a right-angle and to include a very large number of blind approaches. The blind approach arose from the fact that in early days a water-supply for the putting-greens was unknown. Few clubs could have afforded such a luxury, and there also existed a few misguided fanatics who believed that water artificially applied was bad for the turf. Moreover, it was not generally recognised that to import stiffer soil, and thus to form a strong bottom for the grass, would assist the green-keeper to make and maintain a green in a high and exposed position.

Under these circumstances the architect was forced to place all his putting-greens in positions where strong turf could be obtained, and, as such positions were almost invariably hollows, the pot green and the blind approach resulted.

The scheme of taking hazards diagonally instead of at a right-angle has greatly increased in popularity during recent years. There are nowadays a vast number of players who have neither the leisure, the youth, nor the physique which are required in the expert player. It has therefore become necessary to make the game thoroughly interesting, not only for the proficient golfer, but also for players of every handicap, and the diagonal hazard is one of the results.

Some seaside courses still exist on which there are twelve or more blind approach shots, and where the cross-hazards are extremely severe on the duffer while giving the scratch player comparatively little excitement. It is not suggested that these features should be eliminated, but if the members of a club which is reasonably supplied with funds are content to retain a long and monotonous series of them, they do so from choice and not from necessity.

Has Progress been Universal ?

The members of Sunningdale or Walton Heath, of All-woodley or Hopwood, may naturally regard this glimpse of the Victorian Era as a prehistoric peep at a subject which has no more interest for moderns than the sports of the Ancient Briton.

A large number of golfers, however, know by bitter experience that such conditions still exist. The same mistakes in green-keeping may be observed, and almost the same monotony of architecture. The unfortunate players who are doomed to endure golf under these circumstances usually believe that certain expanses of heath and heather, certain tracts of sand-dunes, possess a monopoly of golfing merit, and that their own courses are fated to remain dull and featureless wastes, on which exercise will provide health rather than pleasure.

There is no doubt that sand-dune country is the ideal site for a golf-course, as it possesses certain natural advantages which are not met with elsewhere. The porous sand provides perfect drainage : any grasses which flourish there are of the finest kinds. The undulations are ideal for the game, as they are numerous but not mountainous. Sand bunkers, the finest form of hazard, are ready-made, while long grass, the most detestable, is practically unknown. No worm will live in sharp sea sand if he can help it, and if he does, his sandy casts are a negligible quantity. It must not, however, be supposed that Providence provides a golf-course as a finished article. It is generally necessary to plant a large quantity of bents to prevent the sand from blowing, as otherwise considerable port.ons of the course might be buried to a depth of several inches in a single day. It is also necessary, as a rule, to bring stiffer soil from a distance in order to form a bed for the putting-greens, and some of the fairway may have to be similarly treated. In any case the fairway will require repeated top dressings before it will support turf which is capable of withstanding heavy wear. Except in districts where the rainfall is very heavy, a water-supply for the putting-greens is highly desirable, and this, if it can be obtained at all, often entails considerable expense. If a sufficient amount of turf of a suitable character is not available, it will be necessary to grow turf from seed, and this operation is far more difficult near the sea than it is inland. The high winds which prevail are sure to blow away a good deal of the seed, and it is advisable to start a nursery in a particularly sheltered position, as a reserve supply is always useful for new courses. It is also possible to sow a substantial proportion of perennial rye grass together with seeds of the finer grasses, as this seed germinates very quickly and will furnish a certain amount of shelter for the light and slowly germinating seeds sown with it. The rye grass itself will not survive under seaside conditions for more than two or three years, and in these cases is sown merely for protection. But whatever precautions may be taken, it is by no means easy to obtain a sufficiently strong growth in sand-dune country, unless the dunes have been in existence for many years and are already covered with turf. The suburban golfer, therefore, while conceding the superlative merits of sand-dune country, may console himself with the thought that even in such districts there are special difficulties to encounter. But having admitted the strong points of the good seaside links, and of some of the best heath and heather courses, he may very profitably ask himself whether his own course is as nearly perfect as circumstances permit. It may be of interest to enumerate a few of the questions which may occur to his mind.

QUESTIONS

As regards green-keeping, he will ask whether the putting-greens are as firm and as porous as drainage, sea-sand, and worm-killer can make them, and whether the turf is of fine

2

and even texture ; whether the teeing-grounds and fair-ways remain firm in wet weather. As regards the frame-work and construction of the course, he will ask whether every green is so placed as to take the fullest possible advantage of every natural feature which the land affords ; whether anything has been done artificially to increase the interest of approach play by means of slopes and hollows at any hole which is dull by nature ; whether every bunker is placed and constructed in such a manner as to give the maximum of excitement and the minimum of pain to golfers of every handicap ; whether the course calls for an ample variety of strokes, and whether it is well-planned in relation to the prevailing wind ; whether it has two starting-points, so that players may get away quickly on crowded days ; whether advantage is taken of all available space, so that the line of play to one hole does not border too closely on that to another ; whether the surface of the putting-greens is undulating without being freakish ; whether there are an ample number of positions in which holes can be cut, and whether it is possible to lay the ball dead to these from any part of the green. From the landscape point of view he will ask whether every artificial feature blends with its surroundings ; whether every bunker creates the maximum of impression on, and gives the maximum of thrill to, the mind of the golfer who is seeking to avoid it ; whether the aspect of all the construc-tional work increases the pleasure and stimulates the interest of the golfer who views it. Any player who visits the best of modern inland golf-courses will notice the immense progress which has been made in planning and construction. Inland golf can never be quite equal in merit to that played on sea-side links, but it can be a very good second-best. And it will be realised that, in the keen competition which now exists near the large towns, no club which fails to take ad-vantage of the careful thought devoted to this subject, and approach as nearly as it can to the seaside standard, can hope to remain popular and solvent.

FIFTH GREEN AT MOORTOWN, NEAR LEEDS:
Bunkers and green made out of a flat piece of clay.

EDEN GOLF-COURSE, ST. ANDREWS.
Seventh hole, fairway, and green.

CHAPTER II

THE choice of land for the course and a site for the club house will be dealt with later under the head of Finance, and in considering the present subject it may be assumed that these points have been already settled. The golf-course architect can therefore proceed to fix the positions of the putting-greens and the teeing-grounds.

TWO STARTING-POINTS

His first consideration will usually be to secure two starting-points close to the club house. It is true that at a few clubs which have a small and limited membership this point can be disregarded. But at the average club near a large town there are always a great number of players on Saturdays and Sundays, and most of these arrive at about the same time of day. At many seaside courses also the same conditions obtain during the holiday season, and it is highly desirable that players should be able to start their game as quickly as possible. In many cases also it happens that business men on summer evenings have time for a short round, and this can be played most conveniently on a course where two loops of holes exist, each finishing near the club house. The shape of the available land may, of course, preclude the possibility of arranging for this, but its desirability should certainly be borne in mind.

It is clear, therefore, that one putting-green must, and two should, be placed in the near neighbourhood of the club house, and, if no natural positions exist for them, it will be necessary to construct them artificially. It follows that two lines of play must approach these greens, and space must be left clear for two lines of play to leave the club house. It will also be well to bear in mind that the first hole should be

19

fairly long and fairly easy, in order to get players rapidly away from the first tee. If, therefore, any bold natural features exist in the neighbourhood of the club house, they should, if possible be utilised for some hole which comes later in the round, and it will also be advisable to avoid hugging the boundary at the first hole if this be practicable. It is true that at some famous courses, Hoylake and Prestwick amongst others, balls are frequently sent out of bounds at the first hole, but this feature is not reckoned as an advantage.

To start with an examination of the ground near the club house may seem like putting the cart in front of the horse, but on reflection it will be agreed that an easy first hole, two starting-points and a strong finish are primary considerations, and that it is desirable to form some idea at the beginning of the possibilities in regard to these points.

SITES FOR PUTTING-GREENS

The architect will next proceed to walk over the ground, taking with him a map on which he will note the position of any natural features. In the course of this examination he will record all those sites which Providence has intended mortals to putt on. I have noticed during recent years that mortals have taken very divergent views as to the intentions of Providence in this matter. But this divergence applies to the conformation of the putting-green itself rather than to the ground which lies in front of it and over which the approach shot has to be played. As regards the approach it may be suggested, speaking broadly, that a hollow or ravine, a bank or collection of banks, or a small hill, are the natural features which add interest to the play. The added interest arises from several causes. The player first of all has to consider the trajectory of his intended stroke in relation to the spot on which it will pitch. And the error, if he makes one, is apt to be accentuated by the nature of the ground. For example, he intends to pitch 100 yards on to the top of a hill, and to run twenty yards, the total distance being 120 yards. He does pitch ninety yards (an error of ten yards), but as his ball falls on the upward slope it only runs five yards, and thus stops twenty-five yards short of the objective. Had he made the same mistake on flat ground, the total difference in length would have been very little more than the actual ten yards of error. Conversely, he may intend to play a lower shot in order to pitch below the brow of the hill and run up it. In this case, if he either plays the shot too high or pitches it over the brow, his error is likely to be accentuated.

In the second place he has to be particularly careful to strike his ball truly, because, if he fails to do so, the angle of divergence should be increased by the slope of the ground in front of the putting-green.

In the third place, if his stroke is inaccurate his next stroke will almost certainly be more difficult than it would have been on flat ground.

Apart from these considerations, it is far easier and cheaper to cut artificial bunkers on the face of a natural slope or hill than it is to construct them on flat ground. It is easy to give to such bunkers an impressive and awe-inspiring appearance, and there is far less soil to shift. It is also possible to place and construct them in such a way as to entrap a greater number of bad shots than their actual size and position would appear to warrant, with the result that increased excitement is obtained at a minimum of expense. These considerations have been stated in the baldest terms, but it is probable that any player who thinks of the approach shots which he finds most interesting will realise the importance of such features. It will, however, be recognised that they are intended to add variety to the game, and that, with this in view, it would be inadvisable to eliminate flat approaches, even if it were possible to do so.

THE BLIND APPROACH

It may also, from this point of view, be admissible to endure in the round a blind approach shot played on to a green of the Punch Bowl variety. Many famous courses possess a hole of this description, as, for example, the "Maiden" at Sandwich and the eleventh at Hoylake, and they are as a rule very popular. The objections advanced by some golfers against such holes is that the player loses the pleasure of watching the course taken by his ball after it falls below the intervening ridge, and also that it is not possible to gauge the direction and distance accurately. The latter objection, however, does not always hold good. Take, for example, "Majuba" at Burnham, Somerset, a very good hole of its type. In this case a large sand-hill rises immediately to the left of the green and is visible from the tee, and this gives the player information as to length and direction. In any case the architect need not be afraid to introduce an occasional blind approach, for he will remember that strokes' of this sort are almost always popular, if they do not come too frequently, and also that to ensure variety is one of his principal objects.

It is not by any means every player who will readily notice the positions which adapt themselves naturally for use as putting-greens. There are thousands who will enjoy the finished article for one who will appreciate it in the rough. But the architect who makes the best use of his materials in this respect will greatly enhance the pleasure of the game and will also greatly reduce the expense of construction.

When the chief natural features have been marked on the map it will be possible to consider the framework of the course. It is one of the most delightful features of the game, that the courses on which it is played present infinite variety. Even the best and most popular courses are very dissimilar, and there is no set standard to which it is either necessary or desirable to conform. There are, however, a few points of similarity between most of the good courses, and experience shows that it is well to bear them in mind.

LENGTH

It will probably be agreed that most of the interesting courses are not much longer than 6,300 yards in total length, or much shorter than 5,800 yards, and, although much depends on the amount of run which is likely to develop, it may generally be held that a course which measures about 6,000 yards is well off in regard to length.

When a course is new it will probably be played at its shortest, but it is just as well to have a reserve of length which can be used when the ground has become firm, or in a dry summer. At the same time it is of course true that many courses which are extremely interesting to play on are a good deal shorter than 5,800 yards, and there is no reason whatever why a course restricted in length through lack of space should not provide golf which reaches in quality, though not in quantity, the standard set by a first-class course. The number of short holes which it is desirable to include is a very vexed question. The number of obviously first-rate one-shot holes which it is easy to make is certainly an important factor. But for choice it would probably be safe to make not less than three nor more than five, with four for the happy mean.

It is true that some very fine links, the old course at St. Andrews among them, include only two in the round, but as these holes are always popular, if they are good, it would seem that this is rather a small allowance.

LENGTH OF INDIVIDUAL HOLES

Some years ago it was very much in vogue to talk about good-length and bad-length holes, the implication being that some degree of merit or demerit was inherent in holes of certain measurements. It will probably be admitted that the lengths of the various holes should be such as to incite the player to attempt strokes with every club in a bag of fair capacity ; or, in other words, that an ample variety of length should be secured. But, apart from this consideration, it is doubtful whether any particular length of hole is devoid of interest by reason of its measurement alone. If, however, there is such a hole, it is one which, when at full stretch, is normally just beyond the reach of a well-hit drive struck by a fairly long driver. The length of such a hole, stated in yards, depends on whether it lies up-hill or down-hill, and upon how far the ball may normally be expected to run. But, speaking broadly, it is a hole of not less than 230 and not more than 300 yards. Such a hole may be bunkered either on the assumption that it will not be reached from the tee, or that it will be. If the former course be adopted, the hole will be far too difficult in really dry weather or with a following wind, as many hard hitters (and nowadays there are plenty of these who are nowhere near the scratch mark) will be attempting with a driver an approach planned for a chip-shot. If the other alternative be adopted, the hole will be extremely dull for everyone except the long driver when he has the wind behind him. The ninth hole at Sunningdale, the eleventh at Swinley Forest, and the tenth at Stoke Poges, are instances of this type of hole, and although one example in the round may be admissible for the sake of variety, it is improbable that four or five would be equally popular. Probably the best form of green for such a hole is a plateau, but in whatever way the problem is tackled, it is by no means easy to secure satisfactory results; and, although it would be a simple matter to maintain, on paper, that similar difficulties arise in regard to other lengths, experience seems to show that this particular distance is peculiarly troublesome. In order to secure variety, it would appear that a considerable number of holes should be included which range from 380 to 450 yards, together with a sprinkling of somewhat shorter lengths. The minimum, for choice, will be about 330 yards, short holes excepted. It will of course be understood that if an abnormal amount of run is to be expected, as, for example, in the United States of America, these measurements would be stretched accordingly.

RANGE OF TEEING-GROUNDS

On any course it will be a vital necessity to have a considerable range of teeing-grounds, so that each hole can be readily lengthened or shortened according to the state of the ground, and the strength and direction of the wind. This is a simple precaution which is often disregarded, and even at clubs where ample teeing-grounds exist, it is quite common to find that no intelligent use is made of them. Wind and rain are disturbing factors, and unless the length of the holes is wisely regulated, it is certain that in many cases they will be temporarily robbed of their essential characteristics by the weather.

GENERAL

In evolving his plan, the architect will bear in mind that the majority of his longer holes should not be against the prevailing wind, and the same consideration would apply to really long holes if he decides to include one or two in the round. It is also desirable that he should not arrange too many holes running consecutively in one direction, for in a wind, from whatever quarter it blows, these may become monotonous. In the same way it is preferable that the short holes should face every quarter of the compass in order to secure variety on a windy day. He will also endeavour to avoid skirting a boundary at several consecutive holes, and, if he must do so, he will endeavour to arrange that the out-of-bounds area should not in each case lie on the same flank. If the boundaries have to be skirted frequently during the round, he will try to arrange these holes in such a way that the slice and the pull are equally treated in the aggregate, with perhaps a slight preference in favour of the pull. If any high and steep hills exist on the land, it is desirable to take them diagonally in preference to making a frontal attack. The middle-aged golfer is disinclined for mountaineering in the morning, and, if the house committee know their business, he is even less inclined for it in the afternoon. Large hills of this description are really awkward features in cases where it is necessary to make a putting-green on them in a position which is very much higher than the spot from which the approach shot has to be played. In such cases the putting-green will either be semi-blind but possible for putting, or else visible for the approach but impossible to hole out on. The former alternative is preferable, but it is well to avoid such holes as far as possible, or at any rate to include only one or two in the round. The heights can often be scaled gradually on their less abrupt side, and it is always popular to arrange a tee-shot from a great height downwards. The puniest of drivers, when taking up his stance on such a teeing-ground, will share in fancy the powers of Mr. Edward Blackwell.

The drive and pitch holes may with advantage run slightly, but only slightly, up-hill, and may well be played against the prevailing wind.

Bearing these considerations, and many others, in his mind, the architect may spend interesting hours in an attempt to use the natural features of the land to the greatest possible advantage. Experience will probably teach him that it is often impossible to get every ounce of value out of each individual feature on a good piece of ground, and also that it is bad policy to sacrifice several good holes on the altar of one that is of superlative merit. He will find it necessary to take an all-round view, to weigh the pros and cons of every possibility, and to refuse to be led by a too vivid imagination into any scheme which has brilliant points but is poor in the aggregate. He will also learn that on comparatively feature-less ground it is frequently possible to work in one good feature two or three times, if space permits ; whereas in a scheme less well considered, this feature might have lent interest to one stroke only. It will be generally agreed that intense importance should be attached to utilising every feature in the ground, so far as is compatible with a satisfactory framework. To depend to the maximum extent upon nature, and to the minimum upon art, makes for interesting golf and moderate expenditure.

CHAPTER III

THE PLACING OF BUNKERS

WHEN the framework has been decided upon, the placing of bunkers will be the next consideration. It is no doubt desirable to postpone the construction of some of the bunkers until the course is in playing order. But a course entirely devoid of bunkers would be extremely dull, and moreover some bunkers are necessary for defining the manner in which the various holes should be played and thus bringing out their character. Such bunkers should be constructed in the first instance, especially in the neighbourhood of greens artificially made, the two jobs in these cases being carried out simultaneously. But in cases of doubt it would be advisable to leave the bunkers comparatively remote from the line of play, and to extend them towards the line after the run of the ball has been observed.

Remarks are frequently heard to the effect that "It is wrong to bunker a course for the scratch man," or "We can't bunker this place to suit the duffer." But if every class of player is seeking pleasant excitement, and not a pound of flesh, the conflict of interests should be inappreciable.

COMPULSORY CARRIES FROM THE TEE

One of the greatest stumbling-blocks to the poor player is a compulsory carry from the tee. At some clubs, Swinley Forest and Stoke Poges among others, it is the custom to have two teeing-grounds in use simultaneously, one being a good deal nearer the hole than the other. Players can then arrange, before starting their round, from which of these tees they will play. In this way beginners are saved a great many niblick shots, and they also find it easier to keep their place on the green. From the ordinary tees, however, it will be found inadvisable to arrange many compulsory

27

carries which greatly exceed 110 yards, and I do not consider that the game loses any interest on that account. If the bulk of the compulsory carries were 140 yards, for example, they still would not enter into the calculations of the scratch player unless he was driving against a gale of wind. It is quite true that he might get into a few of them, but this possibility would not be present to his mind when addressing the ball, nor would he enjoy the slightest feeling of satisfaction at carrying them. It is quite possible to give him the advantage which his length deserves without causing the indifferent player to grovel in sand at every hole. It is also, I think, undesirable as a rule to terminate the interest of the hole at the first stroke, which is apt to be the result, if the carries from the tee are too long or the hazards forming them too severe. If one player is hopelessly engulfed off his drive, while the other has reached safety, the latter will either not be called upon to play his second shot, or else be able to poke along in safety without taking the slightest risk. I therefore think that, in order to maintain the interest of the hole to the end, it is desirable that the compulsory carries from the tee should be short, and that at most holes the hazards in front of the tee should not be of too severe a character. A bare chance of recovery may thus be left to the player who has made an indifferent or even a bad drive, and he may at any rate be able to force his opponent to play the second shot correctly in order to win the hole.

A few good players may hold that this is a piece of special pleading on behalf of the duffer, but the majority even of those would probably agree that they do not enjoy any additional pleasure on courses where long compulsory carries are the rule rather than the exception.

OPTIONAL CARRIES

For testing the long driver, and also for putting a premium upon accuracy, it is highly desirable to include a considerable number of long optional carries in the round, and also to provide opportunities for the bold and straight driver to play close past the edge of a hazard which he cannot carry. In all such cases it will be arranged that the player who has brought off the drive successfully should gain a substantial advantage over his more timid or less skilful opponent.

It will also follow that the hazard which may just be carried by the long driver will be on the flank of a shorter player, and thus add interest to both the tee-shots. And it will also result that, although the fairway may be made as broad as space allows, it will be highly desirable to play on to some particular portion of it, in order to simplify the next stroke. It is probable that, while the framework was under consideration, various opportunities for introducing such features were noted, as certain conformations of ground obviously lend themselves to certain types of hole. On the other hand, it is easy to produce similar types of hole on perfectly flat meadows, and although such holes may not be quite so emphasised in feature as they would be on more suitable ground, they will nevertheless provide plenty of interest for every class of player. In the accompanying Diagrams 1 and 2 an attempt has been made to illustrate the possibilities which the expressions "optional carry," "diagonal hazard," and "dog-leg hole" are intended to convey. The holes depicted do not claim to be ideal, nor do they represent a stereotyped pattern which might readily be repeated *ad nauseam*. They are merely intended to suggest certain ideas as to the placing of bunkers with a view to rewarding good golf played by any class of player, and to rendering the game interesting and exciting for all. The general scheme of avoiding long compulsory carries from the tee, and of making the desired direction of the tee-shot dependent on the placing of bunkers near the green, is capable of being worked out in an almost infinite variety of ways which are totally different in fact and in appearance. In Diagram 1 it will be observed that bunker No. 7 is the key to the whole situation, and that bunker No. 1 provides the optional long carry. The remaining bunkers are merely accessory. The long driver, taking the line marked A, has a clear second shot straight up to the hole. He will, however, get a little bit of excitement in steering past bunker No. 7. Player B, who is rather more cautious from the tee, can get somewhere near the green with his second, if he dares to go close enough to bunker No. 7. Player C cannot get anywhere near the green with his second except by a miracle, and will have to play accurately to get a 5. If the shaded portion of the fairway happens to be a deep grassy hollow, the advantage gained by player A would be still further accentuated. It will be observed that the only compulsory carry is for the tee-shot, and that this is less than 100 yards in length.

It is perfectly possible for a very weak player to hole out without having played a niblick shot, though he would no doubt experience some exciting moments before doing so.

Diagram 2 represents a moderate length drive and pitch hole.

DIAGRAM I.

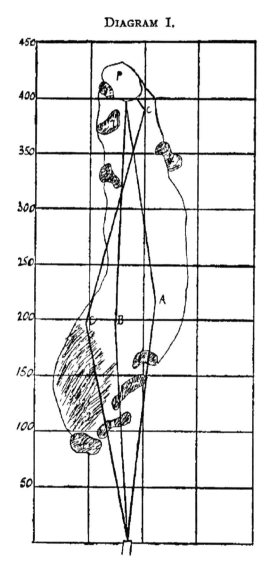

The ground to the left of the shaded line and short of it is a stretch of bent-covered sand-dunes, or of heather-country, or with an " out-of-bounds " angle running along the intermittent line.   The key bunker is No. 1, and for a player of ordinary length the hole is dog-legged by the hazards on the left, while these hazards provide optional carries for the long driver.

Mitchell, playing on the line marked A, makes a carry of 200 yards, and can run up his second if he wants to. Mr.

DIAGRAM II.

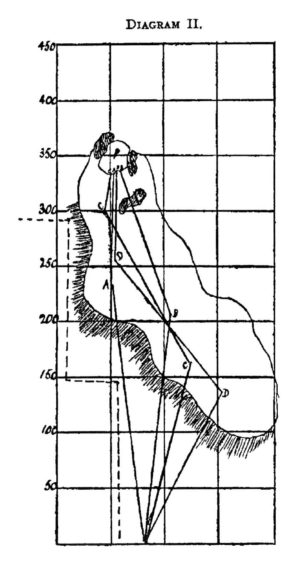

Hilton, driving on the line marked B, makes a considerably shorter carry, but getting his favourite suspicion of " draw," he is very well placed for his second—a fairly simple pitch. Mr. Macdonald, a cautious 10 handicap man, plays a very safe drive on line C. The carry for his second direct to the hole is rather too much for him, nor would he be able to stop the ball on the green if he made the carry with a wooden club. By taking his baffy, however, and making use of his indigenous slice, he may get past the corner of bunker No. 1 and take a wooden putter for his third. Mr. Nicholson, whose handicap has recently been reduced to 16, drives soundly on line D. He is then faced with something of a problem. If he plays his second wide to the right he runs no risks, but his third shot must be a pitch over bunker No. 1, and he does not feel at all confident about it. On the other hand, if he plays to the left to give himself an easy third, a quick hook will land him in the sand-dunes. He decides, however, to avoid the pitch at all costs, and by playing an accurate second leaves himself a comparatively simple third, though his chances of a 5 are by no means so rosy as Mr. Macdonald's. A number of players with single-figure handicaps take a line from the tee which lies between Mr. Hilton's at B and Mr. Macdonald's at C. Those who hit good tee-shots take an iron club for their second and play direct at the hole, with varying degrees of success.

COMPULSORY CARRIES FOR THE SECOND SHOT

The question of a compulsory carry for the second shot is a very thorny problem. All first-rate courses provide some features of this description, though the number of them varies very greatly. The difficulty about introducing them effectively lies partly in the fact that wherever the hazard is placed it means that some players will have to play short, and that this pawky shot is usually considered to be rather dull. If the hazard is so near to the teeing-ground that almost any player of reasonable ability is capable of carrying it with his second shot, the long driver on a summer day will frequently be obliged to take an iron from the tee in order to avoid driving into it. If it is placed so far on as to be quite out of the range of any driver, however dry the ground and however strong the following wind, there will be many days when the golfer whose handicap is in single figures will have to play short of it with his second.

Elasticity of length, however, will to some extent obviate this difficulty, and if a sufficient range of teeing-grounds is provided, it will as a rule be possible to preserve the essential characteristics of the hole in any weather.

Moreover, it is not always easy to play short really well, gaining the greatest possible amount of ground and getting the best available line of play for the next stroke. Such an operation is often a good deal more interesting in real life than it is on paper, and it is improbable that there are many who would wish to eliminate the carry for the second shot, one of the most thrilling strokes in the game, for the mere reason that on occasions a comparatively dull stroke has to be played. A second difficulty in connection with the compulsory carry in front of the green lies in the very great distance which the rubber-cored ball will run in dry weather. It follows from this that at a drive-and-pitch hole a cross-bunker cut so near to the green as to be interesting in winter will provide an impossible shot in dry weather. And conversely, a cross-bunker well placed for summer play will not demand a very fine pitch when the ground is soft. This difficulty is not so pronounced in the case of a somewhat longer hole, where the green committee may well place the hazard well back from the green in a position suitable for summer play. In such cases the second shot in winter will probably be played with a driving-iron or a brassie instead of the mid-iron or lofting-iron which would suffice in dry weather, and the mere carrying of the hazard will in itself provide sufficient excitement for those who are brave enough to undertake it. A further consideration, illustrated by Diagram 1, is that at many holes where no compulsory carry exists it is extremely likely that occasions will arise when a carry or a pitch for the second or some subsequent stroke may become almost compulsory, or at any rate will be a very paying proposition, owing to the inaccurate or timid line which the player has taken previously. On the old course at St. Andrews, where comparatively few cross-hazards exist, an inaccurate golfer frequently provides himself with an opportunity for showing his skill in playing a high dropping shot or using his mashie, and the strokes which he may attempt under these circumstances are of a peculiarly blood-curdling description.

Having indicated some difficulties which attend the introduction of a compulsory carry for the second or some subsequent shot, and having suggested one loop-hole for dispensing with hazards so placed, it may be permissible to urge that a reasonable proportion of such features should be included in the round. The pitch is one of the most beautiful and

3

scientific strokes in the game, and every player, no matter how far or how accurately he is driving, should be encouraged to exhibit his skill in this respect and to reap the full benefit of it. The same consideration applies to the beginner, who will have no incentive to learn this shot if he finds that at every hole he can croquet the ball along the ground with impunity, and he will thus miss one of the pleasantest sensations which golf provides.

The longish carry, also, played up to the green over a cross-hazard, should on no account be omitted, as there is a neck-or-nothing thrill about it which is scarcely equalled by any other stroke, and which is enjoyed by golfers of any handicap, although playing it from very different ranges.

These remarks are not intended to suggest a monotonous series of cross-hazards in front of every green, nor are they written in disparagement of the pitch-and-run approach, a stroke which demands great nerve and skill when played over undulating ground to skirt the corner of a hazard bordering on the line. They are merely a plea for variety, and for providing a test and a reward for skill with every club in the bag.

Diagram 3 represents a hole of the uncompromising drive-and-pitch variety. It will be observed that the hole is most easily approached from the position marked A, as there is a fair margin between bunker No. 2 and the green, and no necessity for playing near bunker No. 4.

OTHER BUNKERS

To obtain this favourable position it is necessary to carry bunker No. 1. Position B may be reached by skirting No. 1 without carrying it, and provides a fairly simple second shot, though not quite so easy as that from position A. Position C is not nearly so pleasant. There is less room to pitch in, bunker No. 4 is unpleasantly close to the line of play, and the stroke is aimed directly towards bunker No. 5. If the shaded portion of the fairway which lies to the left of the putting-green were a mown, grassy hollow, the hole would gain in interest. The approach shot played slightly too much to the left would be shouldered away from the pin, and a comparatively difficult chip would remain for the subsequent stroke. Shots played really wide to the left would provide still more difficult chips. If the ground beyond the green were to fall away slightly, as indicated by the shading, a small but adequate penalty would be imposed upon the overplayed shot on the correct line.   To cut bunkers in the shaded positions would probably be considered to be too severe, and the suggested hollows would provide equal interest and far less agony.

This hole is played over ground which is generally speaking flat, though the putting-green slopes very slightly upwards from front to back, and the ground to the right of bunker No. 1 slopes slightly upwards from left to right.   It will no doubt be realised that a different conformation of ground might considerably modify the bunkering of this hole.   Suppose, for example, that the ground sloped sharply downwards towards the right from the right-hand edge of bunker No. 1. In that case a player who could not carry this bunker would be thrown very wide to the right and would be unable to get the favourable position for his second shot which the present slope of the ground assists him to obtain.   In this case bunker No. 1 would be exposed to adverse criticism, as it would be maintained that the comparatively long driver who could carry it is given an undue advantage.   As things are, the advantage which he gains is appreciable but comparatively slight.   Again, suppose that the ground beyond bunkers No. 2 and 3 sloped sharply downward to the near edge of the putting-green, the present ample space in which to pitch might be hopelessly inadequate on many days in the year. The lie of the land would not favour the construction of an uncompromising drive-and-pitch hole, and in any case the placing of the bunkers would have to be modified.

Diagram 4 represents a two-shot hole which includes a compulsory carry for the second or some subsequent stroke. It is played over ground which is somewhat restricted as to width.   On most days it will be found that the easiest line of play is absolutely direct from tee to green.   With a strong wind from the left, however, many players prefer to keep to the right-hand side of the fairway, as they find that in this way they can more easily avoid bunker No. 6. This hole is of an obvious character but provides excellent sport.   There are a few players who would prefer to see the putting-green more heavily bunkered on the right.   But the slope down into bunker 5 sucks in many sliced and weakly-played shots, and those which are played with sufficient firmness to pass or carry it should hardly be grudged their safety.

It may be worth remarking that, in any case where a bunker borders closely on a putting-green, it is important that the green-keeper should use sound judgment in choosing the position for the hole itself in accordance with the wind and

DIAGRAM III.

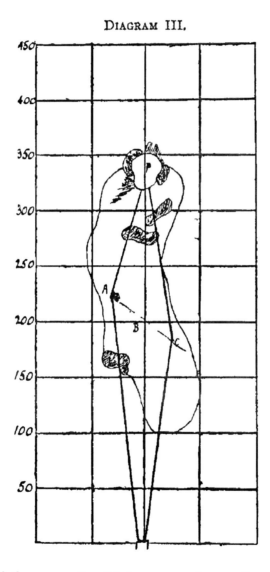

the state of the ground. If, for example, on the green shown in Diagram 3, he cuts the hole on the edge of No. 4 bunker on a day when the ground is hard and there is a strong cross-wind from the left, many players who are brave enough to

LONGNIDDRY, DURING CONSTRUCTION.

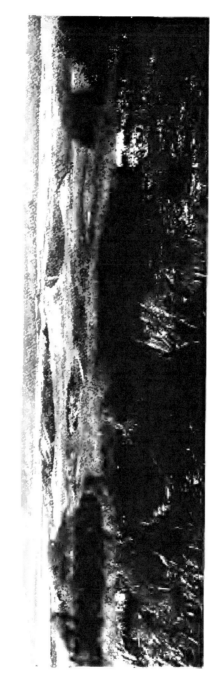

LONGNIDDRY DURING CONSTRUCTION.

try to get near the hole will be bunkered off their very best shots. Similarly, when the ground is hard and there is a strong following wind, it would be a very bad joke to cut a hole on the edge of bunker No. 5. If, owing to wear and tear,

DIAGRAM IV.

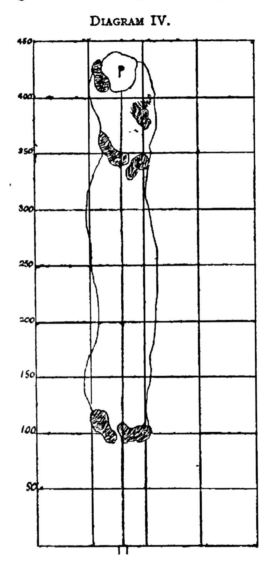

such positions must be used, they should be used when the ground is soft, the weather fairly calm, and when no important matches or medal rounds are being played. To adopt any other method is to kill sport, not to provide it;

by introducing risks which are not worth taking, and by discouraging bold and skilful play.

SHORT HOLES

The placing of putting-greens and bunkers for short holes has not been considered separately, because this differs only in degree from that for approach shots at other holes. But as the player chooses his own stance and may tee his ball, and as all players approach such greens from one fixed point which is chosen from time to time in accordance with the state of wind and weather, it may be permissible to draw in the bunkers rather closer to the hole. For the same reasons it may be desirable to reserve a water-hazard for a short hole if such a feature happens to be available, as more players will have a good chance of negotiating it successfully. It is unfortunate nowadays that comparatively few balls will float, and that there is therefore less chance of seeing a sensational recovery made by means of a stroke played out of water. And a further objection to such hazards lies in the fact that many balls will be lost if the bottom is muddy or smothered in weeds. Some players indeed have an antipathy for water which almost amounts to hydrophobia. But if a clear running stream or a pretty pond with a gravel bed happens to be provided by nature it would be a great pity not to use it. St. Andrews, Prestwick, and Westward Ho! each have their burn, while water-hazards have been utilised on several excellent inland courses for the sake of variety and have proved very popular features.

PROTECTIVE HAZARDS

One other object in the placing of hazards may be termed the " protective," and appears in cases where a comparatively limited amount of land is available. It may under such circumstances be desirable to make a green or tee, or to arrange a line of play, in a position which, though tolerably safe for the players, would not be chosen on land where ample space exists. In such cases an additional degree of safety may be obtained by specially placing bunkers with a view to protection. It may be necessary, for example, to place the tee for the ninth hole somewhat close to the line of play to the fifth. A bunker placed round that side of the ninth tee which faces the players coming up the fifth fairway may not only make them try to steer clear of it, but may also stop a wild shot from landing on the ninth tee. Trees are a fluky and obnoxious form of hazard, but they afford rather good protection, and if a clump of these exists at such a spot it might well be considered justifiable to leave it standing.

It would be necessary to write a very long book, copiously illustrated with diagrams of famous and infamous holes, in order to deal exhaustively with the placing of bunkers. But it is possible that in this essay one or two points have been raised which are of some interest to the average golfer.

CHAPTER IV

CONSTRUCTION

THE subject of construction may be examined from a green-keeping, a golfing, or a "landscape" standpoint. But the first of these aspects is one which does not attract the average golfer. Soils, drainage, climate, grass seeds and manures are topics of technical interest, and the player passes judgment on the results, but has no leisure to study the means by which they are achieved. On the present occasion, therefore, it is intended to regard construction first from a golfing and subsequently from a "landscape" point of view, leaving questions of green-keeping as far as possible in the background.

THE GOLFING POINT OF VIEW—PUTTING-GREENS

The shape, size, and contour of the putting-greens is one of the most important considerations in the game. In constructing a new course or altering an old one it will be necessary to make a good job of these at all costs, cutting expenditure on bunkers through the fairway if necessary. To spend money on making a green which can never be satisfactory is a common form of waste, and to alter it after it is once made is not only extravagant, but also may cause a dislocation of play for a very considerable period. In some favoured spots it is possible to mow out a space which is already covered with suitable turf and possessing suitable gradients and contours, and to work it into good playing order without shifting a barrow-load of soil, sowing a pound of seed, or laying a yard of turf. But more frequently it is necessary to take what nature has provided, and substantially to modify the existing shape and surface of the site before turfing or sowing it.

PINE VALLEY, PHILADELPHIA: FIFTH HOLE.

PINE VALLEY, PHILADELPHIA: TENTH HOLE.

The shape and size of a putting-green is governed by the nature of the stroke which should be played on to it, and by the wear and tear which it will probably have to undergo. Its capacity for withstanding such wear and tear is a green-keeping consideration, but if the club is reasonably provided with funds it will be able to ensure that strength in this respect shall be introduced by art if it has not been provided by nature.

As regards shape, the maximum length of the green will normally run in about the same direction as the stroke which should be played on to it, as the straightest shot will thus have the best chance of remaining on the green, and the minimum of latitude will be allowed to those which are off the line. As regards breadth the maximum may come anywhere, but should normally lie towards the back of the green rather than in front of it. The reason for this is that it is frequently necessary, on account of wear and tear, to make a green slightly larger than is strictly desirable in relation to the approach shot. By keeping the entrance to the green fairly narrow, and making the green itself broaden gradually further on, it may be possible to render the approach shot sufficiently interesting and at the same time to secure a sufficiently large surface for putting. As regards the size of the green, it is clear that, wear and tear apart, a green on to which a fairly short pitch is played might well be made smaller than that which is frequently approached with a wooden club. These considerations are stated in their crudest and widest terms, and are subject to modification in accordance with the gradients in front of the green, and the precise nature of the stroke which should be played on to it. For the same reasons it would be rather unsafe to mention any definite yard measurements, which, while suitable in one position, might be hopelessly unsuitable in another. Speaking broadly, however, it is desirable, if the club can afford it, to make the greens a trifle on the large side in cases where any doubt exists.

There are few things more irritating to a player of any handicap than to judge and strike an approach well and truly, and to feel conscious that he has done so, and yet to find that his ball is not on the green. A pocket-handkerchief green may at the start give a hole a bad name from which it will take years to recover. Moreover, to provide an insufficient margin for changing the position of the pin is to set the green-keeper an impossible task. In such a case no portion of the green will have time to recover from the wear, and the putting will be fluky and unpleasant. In this connection it will no doubt be considered advisable to ensure, as far as possible, that players will leave the putting-green by different routes. It is occasionally observed that the bunkers are so constructed, and the teeing-grounds to the next hole are so placed, as to throw all the traffic over one particular portion of the putting-green, with the result that this portion suffers unduly from wear. In a few cases this may be hard to avoid, but as a rule a little forethought will entirely obviate the difficulty.

The actual conformation of the surface of a putting-green is of vital importance to the game, as it is here that the interest of each hole should reach its climax. But it is a subject which is singularly difficult to discuss in words which bear any precise and lucid meaning.

GRADIENTS

A distinguished golfing journalist recently informed me that the putting-greens of his home course possessed " the three essentials." He spoke of them in a tone which would not have been inappropriate when referring to the Ten Commandments, and I was therefore somewhat reluctant to confess that I did not know what they were. He expounded them as follows :

" 1. It should be possible to cut holes on 75 per cent. of the surface of the green.
" 2. The ball should never gain momentum after leaving the club.
" 3. In holing-out from a distance of 3ft. 6in. it should never be necessary to aim outside the circumference of the hole."

For a moment I was inclined to suppose that this formula was a rather elaborate way of saying that every putting-green should be perfectly flat. But on thinking it over I came to the conclusion that this is by no means the case. Of course a perfectly flat green does comply with its requirements, and in this respect it does not serve as a complete guide. It may also be urged that 75 per cent. of the green

PINE VALLEY, PHILADELPHIA:

The site for the fifteenth tee.

PINE VALLEY, PHILADELPHIA: EIGHTEENTH TEE

is often an unnecessarily large amount of space on which to cut holes; that there is no objection to the ball gaining momentum after it leaves the club, provided that it has scope for losing this momentum before reaching the hole; and that every player ought occasionally to be called upon to aim outside the circumference of the hole when endeavouring to hole out from a distance of 3ft. 6in. But though the formula may be slightly modified to meet the objector on these points, it still forms the basis for a test. Judged charitably in the light of a modified standard, there are many greens now in existence which fail by a wide margin to provide the essentials enumerated. Speaking broadly, the majority of players desire to hole out in two putts on each green if they are putting well. They desire to experience some little difficulty in doing so, because otherwise they would derive no pleasure from success. Therefore a perfectly flat green, or at any rate a series of perfectly flat greens, would not satisfy them.

FREAK GREENS

On the other hand, when they have avoided the bunkers of the fairway, when they have eluded the traps which guard the entrance, and have played their ball on to the putting-green, they do not like to find that it is lying in a severe form of hazard. If a player is conscious that he has gauged an approach putt well and that he has struck it truly he likes to see it go in or dead, and it is nothing but a torment to watch his ball, guided by powers which are beyond his control, go rushing down a steep place like swine possessed by a devil. No amusement can be derived from such incidents, and mortals should bow to the inexorable law of gravity.

Within the limits laid down in this formula, or even in some generous modification of it, the architect may make the putting as difficult as he pleases, though he should be careful to secure that every portion of the greens may be mown easily and without risk of damage.

It may be urged that some existing greens on far steeper gradients than those now indicated, and providing far more numerous and abrupt undulations, have proved universally popular. If this is the case no one would be rash enough to suggest any alteration. But if the architect, when supervising the construction of a new green, is in any doubt as to whether the slopes are of too severe a character, he might do worse than to remember this formula and to consider how far his work diverges from the suggested standard.

THE ENTRANCE TO THE GREEN

The entrance to the green, that is to say the portion of the fairway free from hazards on which the approach shot should pitch, should be an object of considerable care in construction. Thirty years ago this point was almost invariably ignored, and even at the present time it has not always received the attention which it deserves. The consistency of the turf should be such that there is practically no danger of the ball being kicked to one side, or of being unexpectedly pulled up or shot forward. Whether the approach shot be good, bad, or indifferent, it should receive the treatment which it deserves and should obtain the amount of run which its trajectory and spin indicate. There are few things more irritating than to find a stretch of patchy and treacherous turf at the entrance to the green, and in cases where nature has to be assisted in this matter, and the club has sufficient funds, this work should be put in hand in the early days of the course.

On sandy seaside courses the use of light rich soil, and on inland courses the abundant application of worm-killer and sharp sand, are some of the means by which satisfactory results are obtained. And on fat-growing inland courses it is sometimes desirable, if funds allow, to keep the approaches mown by hand. On some excellent courses the approach merges so gradually into the green that it is not altogether easy to say where one begins and the other ends.

The even-handed justice which an approach shot receives when it falls is one of the hall-marks of a first-rate course. It is perhaps more usual to observe this characteristic on a seaside than on an inland course, but many inland courses have attained a very high standard, and many more would do so if they realised the desirability of tackling the job and knew how to go about it.

The undulations which may exist or be constructed at the entrance to a green are of equal importance with the consistency of the turf. In planning the framework, care will have been taken to place each green and approach in the best natural position which is available. But it may still be necessary to eliminate any small and pimply hummocks and to leave either an even surface, or else broad and gradual undulations the effect of which can be easily gauged by the player when making his approach shot. It will no doubt be realised that an undulation, which appears broad and gradual to the man who sees his ball run up close to the pin, may be stigmatised by a golfer who has sliced his approach and been shouldered away from the hole as a small and pimply hummock. In such matters it is better to rely on an unbiassed judgment, as it would be ruin to reduce the entrance to every green to the monotonous level of a croquet lawn.

THE NATURE OF THE HAZARDS

Next in importance is the nature of the hazards, or the character of the artificial bunkers, which should be included in the round. The most common natural hazards are sand, heather, long grass, gorse, and water. Long grass is not an item enumerated in the official list of hazards, but it is an obstacle so frequently met with that it must be referred to here.

The characteristics required of a hazard are that it should be difficult but not impossible to play out of ; that it should not be a cause of lost balls ; and that strokes played out of it should be calculable as regards strength and direction, and should depend for their success on skill and not on brute force alone.

It will be generally agreed that, judged by these standards, sand easily wins the first prize. But it must be light, sharp sand and not clay in disguise. The majority of players will put heather second, provided that it is not allowed to grow too rankly. Long grass is an indifferent form of hazard, but for common use it is perhaps preferable to gorse or water, because a ball, if found, can be played out of it. But brute force is the chief requisite in tackling a shot out of long grass, and such strokes are most exhausting and monotonous if repeated at frequent intervals. On inland courses which are not in heather country it is desirable that fairways should be mown to as great a breadth as funds will allow, and that artificial sand-bunkers should be utilised wherever side-hazards are required. If this is done it will prevent a large number of balls from being lost and thus save much exasperating delay, and it will also provide for the inaccurate player a much more interesting form of recovery stroke. Gorse and water share the disadvantage that it is practically impossible to play out of them, and they are also a frequent cause of lost balls. It would appear, therefore, that they should not be used to any very great extent as hazards if it is possible to avoid this, but that they should be introduced only on rare occasions, for the sake of variety and for decoration.

In making artificial bunkers sand should be used freely if it is available, but an occasional clump of rushes or bents may be planted in positions which favour their growth. These clumps should not for choice be placed close to the edge of a putting-green, because the strength of a stroke played out of them is less calculable than one played out of sand. It is also preferable to use them as side-hazards rather than as cross-hazards, as they would not stand wear.

ARTIFICIAL SAND-BUNKERS

The construction of an artificial sand-bunker is often undertaken in a somewhat haphazard manner, without sufficient consideration of the proper part which it is intended to play in the scheme of the hole.

As regards compulsory carries from the tee, a difficulty confronts the architect, which arises from the resilience of the rubber-cored ball. His desire is to construct these bunkers in such a manner that the player who has driven into one of them shall have a bare chance of recovery. He will, of course, be at a disadvantage as regards his opponent who has driven over them, but, by making an enterprising stroke, he may at any rate be able to compel the other player to play the rest of the hole correctly in order to win it. The architect, while trying to arrange matters in this way, has to remember that, if he trusts to very shallow bunkers with sloping faces, many half-topped shots will jump or run them. This difficulty does not arise in cases where there is a stretch of bent-covered dunes or of heather in front of the tee, but where ground free from such difficulties is being dealt with it has to be faced. A broad stretch of sand helps in pulling up the ball, and it also is desirable that the sand should be well banked up on to the face, so that the ball may stand a reasonable chance of running back a little from it. If this bank is kept well raked up, a good bunker shot will frequently gain an appreciable distance, even though the face above the sand be vertical. It may also be desirable not to cut such bunkers at a right-angle to the line. If they are made in a slightly slanting direction it will help the player to get a little length out of them. And they will not be made deeper than is absolutely necessary. It is no doubt true that, in endeavouring to leave some slight loop-hole for recovery, the architect may now and then be adversely criticised on the ground that his bunkers are occasionally run. And it must be admitted that they will be run more frequently than those which are designed with the sole object of stopping and retaining the ball. But on balance the less severe bunker which leaves scope for enterprise, and does not kill all interest in the hole at the commencement, will be found to be more popular.

The normal object with which the remainder of the bunkers are placed is to introduce an element of risk into the game. The player is tempted to try either to carry or to skirt a bunker. He is offered a reward for success and a penalty for failure. It is evident, however, that the reward and the penalty should bear a due proportion to one another. If the penalty is unduly severe, few players will feel tempted to take the risk ; while if the penalty is almost negligible no daring will be required and no thrill will be experienced.

Broadly speaking, the player does not require to obtain much distance when playing out of a bunker near the green, but must gauge the strength well in order to be quite successful. These bunkers therefore may be comparatively deep, but it should be almost a certainty that a well-played bunker stroke will get the ball out into safety. If this is not the case the sport is not prolonged as much as it should be, for when one player has got into a bunker, which is quite likely to cost him two or three strokes, his opponent will be able to adopt extreme safety tactics, and may to all intents and purposes be able to avoid playing the hole at all. This is a dull game for both sides, and although the player who has not been bunkered himself will rightly play as safely as he can, he will have to bear in mind, if the bunkers are reasonably constructed, that an excess of caution may lose him his apparent advantage.

Similar considerations apply as between the man who has very nearly played the hole well, and his opponent who has played it badly. It may well happen that one man hits a good drive and a second which is almost good. The latter stroke ends in a bunker on the edge of the green. His opponent fluffs his drive just on to the fairway, tops his second just short of a cross-bunker, and plays a moderate third on to the green. The first man is playing the like out of a bunker, and if he makes a reasonable stroke he should be at least as well off as his opponent.

It is no doubt permissible, for the sake of variety, to have one or two particularly obnoxious bunkers in the round. But unless the majority are reasonably easy they will be a toil to the duffer and a very doubtful blessing to anyone.

LANDSCAPE

It is generally recognised that beautiful surroundings add greatly to the attraction of a links. If North Berwick or Rosapenna, for example, could be removed by some super-man or American and set down in a black country among chimneys vomiting smoke, they would no doubt attract the inhabitants by reason of their accessibility: but the crowd which now travels hundreds of miles to visit these places would not take this trouble to play on an equally good course in dreary and unpleasant surroundings.

It is by no means so widely recognised that the " landscape " aspect of actual construction plays an important part in securing the popularity of a golf-course. The appreciation of pleasant surroundings is often subconscious, and many golfers are no doubt under the impression that while they are playing they are entirely engrossed in the game. When they go away to play golf they select a beautiful place for choice, because they realise that, while not playing golf, they will enjoy having something to look at. But, so far as the links is concerned, they imagine that the quality of the golf is all that matters.

It is probable, however, that on consideration they will recognise that this is not the case. Near large towns it fre-quently happens that a piece of ground is chosen for a golf-course which is neither particularly suitable for the game nor particularly attractive to the eye. Such a piece of ground would be chosen because of its accessibility or because it was the only land which could be obtained, and it may very well be the most advantageous position in view of all the circumstances of the case. When the golfer has left a grimy

MADRID: THE FOURTH HOLE.

ROSAPENNA LINKS, CO. DONEGAL.

city for a few hours' relaxation he wishes to find rest and pleasure in the scenery of the country, but it often happens that such a place does not do all that it should to provide him with what he requires.

WHAT TO AVOID

It is a common experience to arrive on a dreary mud flat, broken only by hedges or ditches, and by rectangular cross-bunkers appearing like badly made and badly camouflaged trenches. The fairways run in monotonously straight and parallel lines, and the surface varies mainly according to the length or shortness of the grass. All the constructional work which has been done seems merely to disfigure a landscape which is already dull by nature. Such a spectacle is likely to impose a feeling of depression on a brain which is already tired, and is not likely to enliven anyone, however fresh. This feeling may arise from impressions subconsciously absorbed, and the player may not attribute it to its proper cause, but he must be a very robust and stolid man if he does not fall a victim to it.

For this reason it is suggested that a golf-course should be regarded not merely as an arena for the contest, but also as a property which should be improved in every possible way for the benefit of the club members and their friends. If a beautiful place is to be dealt with, the architect must be careful to improve it; while if the ground is comparatively dull and featureless, he should do all he can to relieve its monotony.

AN OPEN VIEW

In selecting a site for the club house, the view may be only one of several important considerations. But whatever site may be selected, it is highly desirable that the aspect from its windows should be attractive, so that the player may get a favourable impression when he first arrives, and may also get the greatest possible enjoyment out of intervals of rest. To achieve this result it is best, if possible, to create an atmosphere of large and unrestricted space, which is the most delightful contrast to the cramped and restricted streets and offices of a large town.

4

If, therefore, the ground is divided up by a number of hedges, it is desirable to cut all of these down, whether they would interfere with the play or not. The roots can be either grubbed up or mounded over. The ditches can be piped if they are required for drainage, and they can then be either filled in or worked into irregular hollows or mounds.

In cases where the ground is covered densely with trees, it is often possible to open up beautiful views by cutting down a little additional timber. In such cases it would be unwise merely to clear certain narrow lanes which are required for play. The "landscape" effect should also be studied, and although great care must be taken not to expose any unpleasant view in the process, every endeavour should be made to obtain a free and open effect. Swinley Forest, St. George's Hill, and Stoke Poges may be cited as cases in which tree-cutting has greatly improved the views, and in the case of the two first-mentioned clubs a great deal more felling has been done than would have been necessary from a purely golfing point of view.

On the other hand, where very few trees exist every effort should be made to retain them, and in every case the architect will note the quality of the timber with a view to retaining the finest specimens.

Artificial Hazards—Nature the Model

As regards the construction of artificial hollows, mounds, and bunkers, the model should be the natural sand-dune country which is found near the sea.

The most noticeable feature about a sand-dune is that it has a wide base in relation to its height. It will also be observed that dunes are as a rule to be found in ranges, and do not stand isolated in the middle of a plain. They are usually covered with rough grass or bents. Where the sand is exposed it is always in irregular patches, the shape being dependent on the action of the wind.

If the sand-dunes be taken as the natural and perfect model, it follows that their characteristics should be reproduced. Sand-bunkers should therefore be cut in irregular shapes, and should be placed in the face of natural hillocks if these exist in the desired positions. If no banks or hillocks are provided by nature they should be constructed artificially, care being taken to give them a base which is broad in com-

ST. GEORGE'S HILL, WEYBRIDGE:
The first hole during construction.

SUNNINGDALE: THE EIGHTH GREEN

parison with their height, and to make them irregular in outline. Their sky-line should be broken and rolling, and hard, straight lines should be avoided. An excellent effect is produced by banking the sand well up on to the face of a bunker cut in a hillock, so that it is visible at a considerable distance. Similarly, when it is necessary to build up a teeing-ground in order to give a better view of the ground in front of it, it is desirable to create the impression that a hillock existed in the required position and that a teeing-ground has been placed on the top of it. If the top of the artificial hillock is slightly higher than the teeing-ground itself, the flatness and straightness of the teeing-ground will be completely camouflaged, with the result that a hard and unsightly line is entirely avoided.

The work involved in raising the teeing-ground thus adds interest to the aspect of featureless ground instead of disfiguring it.

I can think of one famous course which originally appeared as fifty-seven dreary little fields intersected with hedges and ditches. It now presents the appearance of an open heath, broken here and there with rough and irregular hillocks and hollows among which can be seen patches of white sand, and clumps of gorse and broom. It affords a pleasant and open view, and is equally pleasant to play over.

The same effect could be produced at many other places which now provide a cramped and gloomy aspect. But this side of construction, more than any other, demands in the constructor a natural talent which is very rare, and the majority of courses therefore fall far short of the ideal standard set by nature.

Economy

From the purely golfing point of view, also, it is interesting to observe what very poor results are often achieved at very considerable expense. If a man decides to build a house, and has employed an architect to provide the plans, he does not leave the work of construction in the sole charge of a rather inexperienced bricklayer. This policy, however, is quite common in the case of a golf-course, and the work is frequently left in the hands of men who have either done no constructional work at all, or have in the past obtained very indifferent results. The natural consequence is that, no matter how good the designs may be, a bad and unsightly golf-course is produced and a vast amount of money is wasted.

With wages at their present figure it is improbable that such instances will recur, and committees are now recognising that expert supervision is essential to economy.

CHAPTER V

WHEN starting a new golf-course, or spending a considerable sum of money in altering an old one, it is necessary to examine the financial prospects. Golf has to pay its way, and people who put up the money for golfing schemes are naturally anxious to feel that they will get their money's worth and also that they are likely to receive a reasonable rate of interest.

It is the business of a golf-course architect to pay close attention to this aspect of the matter. In the first place he is in a position to institute comparisons, and in the second place he should be able to sum up the golfing possibilities and to estimate roughly the expense of construction. There are very few people who can accurately appreciate a piece of ground in the rough. To do so requires a special aptitude and a special training. And although members of a committee may be able to gauge the other factors to some extent, it is upon a combination of every factor that success or failure depends.

DEMAND AND SUPPLY

It is assumed that the ground required can be either bought or taken on a long lease, as it would be obviously unwise for a club to spend a considerable sum of money on the course and club house, if their tenure of the land were uncertain or of short duration.

The next question must evidently be one of demand and supply. If no golf-course exists in the district, it is then simply a question whether the golfing population within reach is sufficiently large to support the club. If there are other clubs, it becomes a question whether the golfing population is large enough to support them all, or whether the new club will be so attractive that it has little to fear from competition.

In estimating the golfing population, it is permissible to consider whether a substantial number of beginners are likely to take to the game as the result of forming a new club. This would depend not only on the attractions of the club, but also on the means and leisure enjoyed by a fair proportion of people in the district. Golf is not nowadays confined, as to some extent it used to be, to the classes which have always been devoted to games and sport, and almost anyone who can walk and can afford a subscription is at the present time a potential golfer.

ACCESSIBILITY

The great majority of players are busy men, who are anxious to spend the greatest possible amount of time on the golf-course. They will wish to go there easily and quickly on Saturdays and Sundays, and, if they possibly can, they would like to get a few holes on summer evenings. Accessibility is therefore a very important factor in the success of a club, and there are many cases in which courses constructed on somewhat unpromising sites have drawn a large number of players owing to the ease and rapidity with which they are reached, while others which are greatly favoured by nature have been prevented, by their inaccessibility, from obtaining a large membership. This is more than ever true at the present time, when art can do so much to assist nature; and although a good natural position, other things being equal, is fairly certain to beat a bad one, it is always necessary to remember trains, time-tables, and roads. In this connection the site for the club house itself is a matter of importance. It would no doubt be pleasant to place this in a position which is convenient as regards the planning of the course, and which commands a good view. And it is also necessary to remember the expense of road-making, drainage, laying on water, and the installation of light and the telephone. But ease of access is of primary importance. If, for example, the Sunningdale Club House, which is five minutes' walk from the railway-station, had been built on the hill behind the fifth tee, the members would have had two starting-points, and an even more charming view than they now possess, being surrounded entirely by their own golf-course. On the other hand, they would have lost money over building expenses, road-construction, and water-supply, would probably have had a fair amount of traffic crossing their second hole, and would have burdened the traveller from London with extra expense and waste of time.

THE QUALITY OF THE GOLF

There can be little doubt that the golfing public is more critical of golf-courses than it used to be. More good courses exist now than formerly. Indeed, thirty years ago a really good inland course was practically unknown. It follows that the standard of comparison is higher. It has also come about that golfers travel more and see more courses than they formerly did, having at their disposal either the motor-car or a much improved train service. A critical eye is not confined to the few who are experts at the game, and almost every player at the present time holds strong opinions as to the merits and demerits of each course which he plays over. It follows, therefore, that the quality of the golf is the foundation on which the success of a golf club must be built, and no club can afford to disregard this consideration. A good natural site is greatly to be desired in this connection, but, if this cannot be found, a great deal can be done with brains and an adequate supply of money.

OTHER ATTRACTIONS

Golf is no doubt the chief reason why people join a golf club. But auxiliary attractions may form a deciding factor in the success of a club which does not possess a golf-course of outstanding merit. It sometimes happens that the wife of a golfer does not play golf herself, and it also happens, especially in summer, that the golfer does not want to spend the whole day on the links. Beautiful surroundings are at all times desirable, but in such cases as these a shady garden and a few lawn tennis courts may make all the difference. I am a little doubtful as to whether a squash racquet court or a swimming-bath would repay the expense of construction, but there can be no doubt that a comfortable card-room is a great asset, especially on a wet day.

It may also be observed that golf, however badly it may be played, seldom brings on a loss of appetite The house committee therefore have an important part to play, and may compensate the member to some extent for his sufferings at the hands of the green committee. No one would be so rash as to suggest that potted shrimps or a baron of beef, or even nourishment of a more soluble character, have been responsible for the success of the Royal Liverpool Golf Club. The golf at Hoylake stands on its own merits. But the visitor who has enjoyed these things will be unlikely to remember any of his bad shots, and may even fail to recollect his good ones.

The considerations which affect holiday or seaside courses are very similar to those already enumerated. But in such cases the question of accessibility often becomes a question of hotels, lodging-houses, or a dormy house. Demand and supply can be treated on rather wider lines, but the quality of the golf and other attractions remain a deciding factor. In judging the financial prospects of a club, many other points have to be considered. But the few which have been raised here may indicate that an all-round view must be taken, and that one consideration must be weighed with another if a correct estimate is to be formed.

Conclusion

These essays have not been written to defy the expert or to instruct the novice. They are merely intended to suggest to the average golfer certain trains of thought, or points for debate, which may stimulate his interest in the courses on which he plays.

CHAPTER VI

LABOUR-SAVING MACHINERY AND THE COST OF CONSTRUCTION

By Dr. A. Mackenzie

THE difficulties arising from the demands of labour for higher wages and shorter hours are only to be surmounted in golf-course construction, as in most other industries, by better methods of organisation and by labour-saving machinery.

On some courses which have been constructed under my personal supervision, I have actually had better results with less cost since the Armistice than before and during 1914.

This has been partly due to increased experience whilst engaged in somewhat similar work during the war, but is to a greater extent owing to the fact that green committees and green-keepers show much less opposition to the adoption of new methods and labour-saving machinery. They are willing to give any new idea a fair trial and pay a fair price for its introduction.

The machines I have found most valuable in golf-course construction are the mole-drainage machine, the turf-cutting machine, and the American scraper or scoop.

MOLE-DRAINAGE MACHINE

There is nothing new about a mole drain, which has been in existence for many years. The old methods of using it, however, were expensive and cumbersome, and it gradually fell into disuse.

Formerly two large traction engines were required, and this had many disadvantages. The cost of bringing these engines to the site was only warranted when an extensive area had to be drained; and it was not easy to obtain all the necessary machines on hire. It was almost impossible to bring them on to boggy land, and if you succeeded in doing so their weight broke all existing drains. About twelve years ago Franks, the Moortown green-keeper, and I devised a mole drain which could be readily drawn by horses or a small tractor. This was a great success in every way, the land being drained very effectively and cheaply. The good results of the drainage have already lasted for twelve years.

The mole is a torpedo-shaped instrument and is attached by a knife to a carriage moving on wheels. The carriage is drawn by horses or a small petrol tractor. The instrument burrows under the ground like a mole, and the only disturbance of the surface is the small cut made by the knife. This small incision does not interfere with the play, and is hardly noticeable in two or three days. The mole drain must be united to an existing drain, stream, or ditch, and it is usually advisable to pipe the junction between it and the main drain.

The action of the mole is to push the clay to each side, compress it, and form a channel like a drain-pipe which remains patent for many years.

The best results are obtained in heavy clay, but I have also found it beneficial in loam. It aerates the ground and allows the water to percolate through quickly.

COMPARATIVE COST OF MOLE DRAINAGE

The cost depends on the facilities for hiring a tractor, the presence of existing drains, and on the lie of the land. On the last golf-course I kept a record of, the mole drainage was done at one-twelfth of a penny a yard. Drainage with three-inch pipes would have cost a shilling a yard. This works out at one 144th of the cost of tile draining. In addition to this it is necessary to construct main drains when there are none in existence. It would not be unfair to estimate the cost at an average of one-twentieth to one-fiftieth of that involved by the usual methods.

To drain a clay course of 100 acres by ordinary methods as efficiently as is necessary for golf would cost about £3,000. Mole drainage would perhaps cost £100.

The number of the main drains, the depth and size of the mole drain, the necessity of additional pipes, and the question of cross-drains depend on the lie of the land, the character of the subsoil, etc. Experience is a valuable guide in getting the best results with the minimum of cost. But there can be no question that a skilful use of the mole drain in clay

TURF-CUTTING MACHINE AT WORK.

THE SCRAPER CONVERTING THE FLAT INTO UNDULATING LAND.

or heavy loam will produce some of the physical characteristics of sandy soil. The water percolates through the surface at once, and the result is that all muddiness and stickiness are eliminated. The character of the grasses entirely changes, and the fine golfing grasses are encouraged at the expense of the coarse agricultural grasses. Even the worms vanish, the ground becoming so dry that they cannot work in it. The advantages claimed for mole drainage in distinction to other methods are cheapness, the conversion of muddy and worm-infested courses into good winter links, the encouragement of fine golfing grasses, the non-interference with play while the work of drainage is being carried out, and the rapidity with which good results are obtained.

THE TURF-CUTTING MACHINE

The machine in common use was made according to my design. One horse is sufficient to cut the turf on most soils.

The machine is constructed so that there are two circular knives to do the side-cutting, and two horizontal ones for the under-cutting. After completion the turf lies in long ribbons on the ground, and can then be cut into suitable lengths and removed. The blades can be adjusted so that the sods may be cut to the depth desired. It is essential that it should be manipulated by a man who is accustomed to the use of a plough.

On those rare occasions when complaints have been made as to its efficiency, I have invariably found either that the blades have not been adjusted correctly or that it has been condemned by a man who was unfamiliar with the handling of a plough.

COMPARATIVE COST

One man, a horse, and the turf-cutting machine, may under favourable circumstances nick and pare an acre (4,840 square yards) of sods per day, whereas by hand a man rarely cuts more that 240 square yards per day. The cost therefore amounts to about one-eighth of that for the usual method, while the sods are cut at a more even thickness and are easier to lay.

THE SCRAPER OR SCOOP

The scraper or scoop has been extensively used in America and Canada, but very rarely in this country. It is shaped like a huge shovel with handles and is worked by two horses. After the sods have been cut by the turf-cutting machine and the turf removed to one side, the scraper is used. The man in charge takes hold of the handles and the scoop is dug into the ground, the horses pull and the scoop is filled with soil. The handles are then depressed and the scoop is allowed to slide on its bottom to the required position, when it is tilted up.

An economical way is to employ four scoops on the same green, hummock, or bunker. One man can then do all the filling for the four scoops, and another all the tilting.

The scoop can be used in any soil except rock or gravel. In heavy soils it is necessary to plough the land layer by layer before the scoop is used.

COMPARATIVE COST

The cost depends on the nature of the soil. My impression is that, comparatively speaking, one gets better results on heavy soil than on sand, notwithstanding the fact that the land has to be ploughed before the implement is used. The average man can dig three times as much in sandy as in heavy soil, but the difference is not so much when the scoop and plough are used.

The cost is roughly one-fifth of that for ordinary methods. One of the advantages of the scoop is that it is difficult to make hummocks of an unnatural appearance with it. The hummock must have a gradual slope, as otherwise the horses would not be able to climb up it readily. Another advantage is that the weight of the horses compresses the hummocks and prevents them sinking so much after they are turfed.

GENERAL

It will no doubt be recognised that the use of these mechanical implements is not possible on every soil, and that, even where they can be employed, the method of use and the results obtained will vary. It is necessary to consider the nature of the site and of the soil in each individual case, and it may easily happen that an implement which is very effective on one part of a course may be quite useless on another.

It is not therefore suggested that they should be universally adopted, or that they will produce good results under inexperienced direction. On the other hand, it is highly desirable, in the interests of economy, that the subject should receive due consideration.

CHAPTER VII

GOLF IN BELGIUM

By Lieut.-Colonel F. T. Bacon, Secretary of the Knocke-sur-Mer Golf Club

AT the present time Belgium possesses more than one golf-links famous in the golfing world, but it is only a comparatively short time ago that the Royal and Ancient game was practically unknown in that country. Probably the first golf played in Belgium was played at the now well-known and popular watering-place, Knocke, which at that time, however, was nothing more than a tiny little fishing village, lost among the bleak and wind-swept dunes of the Belgian coast. In the year 1899 a few English people residing at Bruges began to come out to Knocke to practise golf among the sandhills; their course was primitive in the extreme: the holes consisting of " jam jars " sunk in the ground with the aid of a trowel, and a local peasant with a large pair of scissors being employed to cut the longer grasses within a foot or so of the hole, the clearing thus made doing duty as a green.

Time passed, and by degrees a few Belgians who came to Knocke occasionally for the bathing began to take an interest in the game; and in 1901 a club was formed, a mowing-machine purchased, and three years later C. Warren was engaged as professional, and has been at the club ever since.

Following swiftly on the inauguration of the Knocke Golf Links, clubs began to spring up all over Belgium. A good story is told of the late King of the Belgians in connection with the opening of the links in the Forest of Sognie: His Majesty was one day receiving a newly-arrived American ambassador, and in the course of conversation happened to ask him what he thought of the country. The representative of the United States confessed that so far he had not been very favourably impressed, as it had rained ever since his arrival, and worse still, he found himself deprived of his

Mr. H. S. Colt.   Mr. C. Harris.   Sertond.   Mons. H. Cachard.

GROUP TAKEN AT THE ST. CLOUD COUNTRY CLUB, PARIS.

KNOCKE: SECOND GREEN ON BIG COURSE.

favourite form of amusement, as there was no golf-links.
Leopold II replied that he regretted his inability to influence
the weather, but that he could and would supply the remedy
to the second objection. The King was as good as his word,
and gave his beautiful shooting-box of Ravenstien, in the
Sognie Forest, for the purpose, whereupon it was transformed
into the Royal Belgian Golf Club, which now has a summer
course at Le Coq, a few miles from Ostend.

About 1908 a golf-links was laid out in Ghent and another
at Antwerp. Nieuport, realising how much golf had assisted
the development of other places and not wishing to be out-
done, laid out a good links at Lombartzyde, which was rapidly
coming to the fore, but which has, unfortunately, been completely destroyed during the war. Spa has recently added a
golf-links to its long list of other attractions, and it is fast
becoming an absolute necessity for any Belgian town, which
wishes to keep pace with the times, to be able to offer good
golf within a reasonable distance.

While all this activity was going on in other parts of Belgium,
the pioneer course at Knocke was not allowing itself to be
outdistanced by the newer links. Much had happened since
the days of the 10-inch mowing machine and the jam-jar
holes ; the links became yearly more popular, and the seaside
resort of Knocke Zoute grew and prospered with it. In
1909 the increasing number of golfers who came as visitors,
and the fact that the land upon which the course was laid out
was required for building purposes, necessitated its removal
to a better and more sheltered site a short distance farther
inland. The new links were no sooner opened than they
were crowded with visitors who flocked from all parts of
England and Belgium to enjoy some of the best golf to be
had on the Continent.

The tiny fishing village of ten or twelve years before had
become one of the most flourishing watering-places on the
Belgian coast. To give some idea of the expansion necessitated by the rush following on the opening of the new course,
it is only necessary to state that over one hundred hotels
and boarding-houses were built during one winter, and the
following summer they were all filled to overflowing almost
immediately.

A new club house was built in a commanding position,
on a very large dune overlooking the links, and in 1910 the
course again became so overcrowded that the committee

of the club decided to make a second course, and also to carry out some radical improvements in the existing one, which had originally been laid out by amateurs. The club was fortunate enough to secure the services of the famous expert, Mr. H. S. Colt, who came over from England and laid out two 18-hole courses, with the result that Knocke became possessed of a links which was second to none on the Continent. In the following year even more English people came over, attracted by the new courses, to which was now attached the added distinction of being laid out by Mr. Colt. Belgian and French golfers also came in large numbers, and it would only be stating a bare fact to say that Knocke owes its present prosperity almost entirely to its golf-links.

The coast of Belgium, consisting as it does of sandhills, with intervals of short springy turf between them, is particularly well suited to the game of golf, and the links in this neighbourhood are eminently sporting ones. As yet there are comparatively few courses on the Belgian littoral; but given money and sufficient enterprise, there are golden opportunities and unbounded possibilities for the laying out of several more first-rate golf-links on what is at present the waste land of the district.

This part of Belgium is yearly becoming more and more popular, and there are many growing colonies of English people who have settled at various places along the coast. The Belgian watering-place offers all the advantages and none of the disadvantages of the English seaside resort. The proverbial " tripper," with his orange-peel and paper bags, is almost a thing unknown; the accommodation is good and the living extraordinarily cheap; the bathing is as good as any that can be had in England, and there are many excellent tennis courts. Over and above all these, to many people minor advantages, there is the splendid golf, to which several of the towns owe their prosperity almost entirely. Altogether it would be almost impossible to find a locality more ideal for the retired officer, or civilian of moderate means, who wishes to enjoy a good summer holiday without incurring too much expense. He will be able to find twice the amount of amusement at about half the cost of a holiday in England, and should he wish to settle down, as so many do who have once enjoyed a few months on the Belgian coast, he will find many charming sites from which to choose one, where he can build a villa in any style which he may personally prefer.

CHAPTER VIII

OTHER OPINIONS

MR. F. J. MORRISON, the Honorary Secretary of the Hamilton Golf and Country Club, Hamilton, Ontario, in writing to Mr. Colt in August 1919 about the International Match, which had recently taken place between teams representing the United States of America and Canada, on the links of that club, laid out by Mr. Colt in 1914, stated that Mr. J. C. Fownes, captain of the U.S.A. team, in referring to this course, spoke in terms of praise but thought that more bunkers were needed. Mr. Morrison further mentioned :

" I think it quite likely some trapping may be required, but we are not going to have any amateur work and probably be let in for one change and another which we should like to undo. The course will stand as it is until you can come out here. Now that the war is over I hope that we may expect you on this side not later than next year.

" I hope you won't think it purely ' blow ' when I say that we have nothing so good in Canada in the way of a course, not many as good in the States and few better."

M, H. Cachard writes to Mr. Colt :

" In answer to your letter :

" The start that golf had made in France was checked by the war, and as far as I know no new course has been made during the last five years ; on the other hand, of the existing courses some have been requisitioned, some have been more or less damaged, and others insufficiently attended to. In all cases the work of renovation has been begun, and will be rapidly completed. The St. Cloud Country Club was opened some months before the outbreak of the war, and in spite of all the difficulties we have had to surmount, we never ceased to work at the improvement and embellishment of our property.

" Our 18-hole golf-course, so cleverly laid out by you, is in excellent condition, and the admiration of players, including the best known professionals. We have just completed our supplementary course of 9-holes, which you also planned, and which will be a great attraction.

" From next spring our members will have at their disposal three

9-hole golf-courses of which you know the charm, a magnificent polo ground, tennis courts, and other games. What efforts it has cost to obtain these results ! A few years ago the Parc de Buzenval, containing 70 hectares, was an uncultivated forest in which the brushwood was so dense it was impossible to judge the configuration of the ground. We had to cut down more than 10,000 trees—oak, beech, chestnut, birch—and as they fell we had to get rid of their stumps, digging deep holes to bury the largest of them.

" Our country club is admirably situated on one of the highest slopes of the outskirts of Paris, only two miles from its gates, where one enjoys a superb view of all the surrounding district.

" Since the opening of the club members have flowed in, and the actual number of members is now more than 1,100.

" Many of our members who we had not seen for five years, as they were serving in the army, have now taken up their old habits and play golf regularly. Young people have learnt the game, and we shall soon have at St. Cloud a clan of good players who will be able to figure honourably in competitions. Golf tends to become more and more popular in France, and I believe that many new clubs will be started all over the country. As to the clubs which already exist, they will benefit by the experience they have gained, and will know how to offer more conveniences to their members. In a word, I believe that a bright future is reserved in France for the ancient and noble game of golf."

Mr. Horace Hutchinson writes to Mr. Colt:

" I am very glad to hear from your letter that you are resuming your beneficial pre-war activities as course constructor, and are forming yourself, as I understand, into a company, with Captain Alison and Dr. Mackenzie for your co-directors. It ought to make a very useful firm, and I may say at once that I am as full as I can hold with gratitude for all that you and others have done in the past, in the way of transforming the most unlikely-looking land into golf-courses. I am old enough to remember a time when we used to say that golf, real golf, could not be played on inland soil. You have gone far to change all that.

" At the same time, since your letter lays open the door of invitation to criticise, I will say that in my humble opinion one of the points to which you links-makers have not given quite enough attention is the distinction that I should like to see made between bunkers ' through the green ' and bunkers ' guarding the putting-greens.' These latter, as I think, should be made deep with a steep cliff so that the niblick has to dig deep to get the ball out of them, and it should have to be a good dig at that. But the bunkers through the green I do not think should be of quite equal depth, nor of such steep faces. If you made these ' through the green ' bunkers deep pits, you then reduce all and sundry who get into these to a monotonous equality, for even the best bunker player, as the worst, has equally to dig—practically to lose a stroke. If, on the other hand, you have these bunkers rather shallower, with cliffs not quite so high, and broken here and there, you then give a good bunker player, a man who is an adept at making the best possible out of a bad lie, a fair chance of getting the equitable

HAMILTON, ONTARIO: THE ELEVENTH TEE.

TORONTO GOLF-COURSE, CANADA:

advantage of his skill. He will very likely be able to get the ball a considerable distance out of such a bunker, far enough, perhaps, to save him a stroke in reaching the green, whereas the other man in the same situation, who was not an expert in bunkers, would not get his ball so far; and would probably lose a stroke, in reaching the green, to the other man. You induce the more daring players to take a sporting risk, with a view of getting distance out of the bunkers; with the deep bunkers through the green, it is a simple matter of loss of stroke for good and bad alike.

" That is the first point that I would humbly suggest to you.

" Then a second is that you might make an occasional use of what I would call the ' bottle-neck ' approach to the green, with the bottle and its neck set at something like a right-angle to the direction down which the ball has to be driven. My point is that you should so arrange the hazards guarding the green, that a man should be obliged to get his ball to a certain place down the course, so far and no farther, in-order to give himself the clear approach up the neck of the bottle. If he did not get just to that spot, he should have a shot almost impossibly difficult to play, so as to give due advantage to the man who played accurately enough to find himself just opposite the clear neck of approach. And I would make the green so difficult and so well guarded that it would be virtually impossible for a man to stop on it with a full shot even if able to reach it. Of course I am not suggesting this as the kind of hole that should come in often; but I do think that once or twice in the round it would be rather a good novelty and a searching test of accuracy of play.

" Then, when you have finished your course-laying, and are going home to enjoy some well-earned repose, you will, I presume, together with your blessing, leave some instructions for the green-keeper. Now, the green-keeper on many of the links and courses that I have seen has erred in this : that he has cut his putting-greens out in form of a regular square. He has perhaps made them very nice to putt on within this square area, but the result is that, if you are approaching from, say, a hundred yards, you are obliged to pitch the ball not at any prepared ground at all, but on what is virtually the rough and natural ground of the course I am presuming, obviously, that the putting-green is not of such extravagant size that you are able to pitch right on it and stop there. That may, indeed, be possible for a man who is very adept at putting cut on the ball in the event of the ground being sodden with rain, with wind blowing in force in his face, but in normal conditions it should not be possible even for the most expert. In these conditions all that remains for a man to do is to pitch the ball up into the rough on the edge of the green and take his chance of what happens to it on alighting. It may pitch on a lump which will stop it dead, or it may pitch on the downward further slope of that same or another lump, in which case it will go shooting over the green. The best he can do is to strike an average and trust to luck.

" This is not as it should be, nor as it need be. The man of ordinary skill in pitching should have ground on which to pitch that he can trust. He should be able to play the stroke in the confidence that his ball will get fair treatment on alighting, and he ought to be able to make a tolerably good estimate as to the amount of run that it will have on it after pitching. And to ensure all this you do not need to instruct the green-keeper to mow a larger area. All you need to do is to tell him to alter the shape of that area from the square to the rectangle.   Let him make the putting-greens narrower if you like— most greens are on the side of being too broad—but let him carry the green and the mown and rolled ground a little farther away from the hole, and towards the place from which a man who is playing the hole correctly will approach it.   Then his pitching need be no longer of the ' chuck it and chance it' order ; he will know fairly well where his ball is going when it lands, and the expert will gain the due advantage from his skill, of which he is defrauded when the ground on which his approach shot has to fall is so rough no reliance can be placed on what will happen to it.

" And finally, I think you might impress this further plain truth on your green-keeper, because comparatively few act as if they had any appreciation of it : that greens vary, and that according to their variety should be the rolling and mowing to which they are subjected. They vary, for one thing, in their gradient ; you yourself are an artist in the cunning contrivance of gradients ; and sure, in very mercy to the putter, it would be well to instruct your green-keeper to allow the grass to be a little longer on the more sloping than on the nice level greens   A level green like that of the Hole O'Cross at St. Andrews may be as fast as you please, but if you had the same keenness and the same bareness on a green of the slope of the eleventh, the short hole coming in, the ball would never stay on the green at all.   It would roll down into Strath's bunker, even if you laid it on the green by hand. Some greens, moreover, are more exposed to the wind than others, where you cannot afford to shave as closely as where the putter is tolerably sure to be doing his delicate work in a calm.

" In some aspects and in some soils, the grass naturally asserts itself more than elsewhere ; and these varieties of condition you may often find within the limit of the same course.   All that is known to you far better than it is to me ; but it is not, as it appears, known as it should be to every green-keeper.   Therefore, I say, impress it upon his attention, and also on the attention of any of the green committee who do not deem themselves too wise to receive counsel.

" That is my last word, and I have to apologise for the many that have gone before it."

Mr. John L. Low writes :

" The architect has been the best friend that golf has had during the past few years.   The game has been waging a battle against the inventor, and the architect has come to its assistance.   The one aim of the inventor is to minimise the skill required by the game : he tries to invent something which will make skill less necessary ; he appeals to the skill-less player and offers him something ' much easier to play with.'   The inventor has been allowed too much licence, and but for the counteracting influence of the architect the game would have been entirely emasculated.

" No game depends so much as golf on its arena for success : on an interesting course an interesting game will be played ; on a badly planned green the game will be dull.

" The trick of the thing is to make the ground dictate the play. The shot from the teeing-ground is nearly always far too wide : it is a case of driving anywhere straight ahead.   The good architect will see to it that the hole proclaims that you must keep well to the left, or well to the right, as the case may be. And so in each stroke in the round there should be some special interest which demands some special manœuvre.

"Strange to say, very few people have this trick of giving character to a hole, though every golfer is willing enough to offer advice. It is largely a matter of experience: success comes through the real cause of previous failures. Mr. Colt and a few others who have devoted themselves to this important part of the game have developed a special sense which enables them at once to see the weak point in a hole and know how to strengthen it. It is not a matter of rules, it is a gift. But at the back of it there must lie the sure basis which is formed by a complete knowledge of the many varied strokes which make up the content of the game."

Mr. "Chick" Evans writes:

"I remember Dr. Mackenzie and Captain Alison. They ought to make splendid partners. I know your booklet on Golf-course Architecture will be one of the most valuable ever gotten up.

"I am glad to know that such fine associates are going to give the golfing world a book on Golf-course Architecture. If there is any subject upon which there is more of a diversity of opinion between green-keepers, in the golfing realm, I do not know it. Thousands upon thousands of players have been working in the United States to better golf-course upkeep and architecture. I know green-keepers who are posing as experts who are practically the same as thieves. They spend the club's money on their wild ideas, and no good results from it. Your book will be most enthusiastically read by me.

"It is nice to know that the golf-courses on the other side are being fixed up to their pre-war condition. There is a great deal of work that you could do over in this country"

Sr. Duque de Alba, writing to Mr. Colt in August 1919, says:

"I am only too pleased to give you some news of our ' Real Club de la Puerto de Huero,' where the links that you laid out have been a very great success.

"The club is flourishing. From 290 members in 1913, we have gone up to over 600, and the club-house is now being enlarged to suit increased members An electric tram runs right up to the gates, six tennis-courts have been built, and polo, golf, and tennis have been played all through the War

"Golf is so popular now that last spring there were days when over 100 players went round in a day.

"All our greens have plenty of water, and the supplies are excellent. We are now irrigating most of the fairways, and trying in time to have good lies all round, even during dry seasons.

"Owing to the increase of players, the entrance fee has been put up to 250 pesetas. The subscription is 180 for tennis and golf and 350 for polo players. Foreigners pay 50 pesetas per month and no entrance fee."

Fifty Years of Golf

By HORACE G. HUTCHINSON.

Freely illustrated. 10s. 6d. *net; by post,* 11s.

"Mr. Hutchinson's reminiscences, with their many illustrations, will interest every golfer, for he is the leading authority on the rise of golf in England."—*Spectator.*

Pastime with Good Company

Pictured by G. D. ARMOUR

With an introduction by HORACE G. HUTCHINSON.

Royal quarto, tastefully bound, gilt, 18s. 9d. *net; by inland post,* 19s. 6d.

Containing over Fifty Choice Plates,
Thoroughly typical of Mr. Armour's Art.

"A book for every sportsman's library."—*Liverpool Courier.*

Fishing

Edited by HORACE G. HUTCHINSON.

In 2 volumes, each 15s. 8d. *net; by post,* 16s. 6d.

The Fishing Gazette says:—"I know pretty well every book in our language, and in French and German, on the subject of Fishing, but I know no work which is so good, comprehensive, and cheap as this. Would be worth buying if it were merely for the illustrations."

Animal Life by the Seashore

By G. A. BOULENGER, LL.D., D.Sc., Ph D., F.R.S., and C. L. BOULENGER, M.A., D Sc.

An indispensable handbook to all who wish to increase their knowledge of the habits and life-histories of the wonderful creatures which are to be found on our seashores. Nearly 100 illustrations.

Large 8vo. 6s. 3d. *net; by post,* 6s. 7d.

The Yorkshire Observer says:—"Such a book was sorely needed, for almost all the works of a popular character dealing with shore life are sadly out of date."

The Horse and the War

By Captain SIDNEY GALTREY.

Beautifully illustrated by Captain LIONEL EDWARDS, with a note specially contributed by Field-Marshal Sir DOUGLAS HAIG, K.T., G.C B., etc.

Crown quarto, 6s. *net; by post,* 6s. 6d. *In special binding,* 10s. 6d. *net; by post,* 11s.

"Few of us realize the debt we owe to the horse and the mule and to the men who fitted them for their task. In any survey of the thousand wonders of the last four years this book must take a place."—*Glasgow Herald.*

Our Common Sea-Birds

CORMORANTS, TERNS, GULLS, SKUAS, PETRELS, AND AUKS

By PERCY R. LOWE, B.A., M.B., B.C.

With Chapters by BENTLEY BEETHAM, FRANCIS HEATHERLEY, W. R. OGILVIE-GRANT, OLIVER G. PIKE, W. P. PYCRAFT, A. J. ROBERTS, etc.

Large quarto, cloth, gilt, with over 300 *pages and nearly* 250 *illustrations.* 18s. 9d. *net. Post free (inland)* 19s. 6d.

Unlike the majority of books dealing with birds, this volume is of interest to the general reader and to the student of ornithology alike.

It is a book that enables the reader to identify our Sea-birds by name, to understand their movements, their habits, their nests and their eggs.

The Observer says :—"We marvel at the snapshots that have been taken of birds. Every movement of their flight is now recorded; the taking off, the alighting, the swooping, the settling, the 'planing,' the struggling against the wind. And they are just the birds which the ordinary man wants to know about, because he has such opportunities of seeing them for himself on any walk along the cliff."

The Peregrine Falcon
At the Eyrie

By FRANCIS HEATHERLEY, F.R.C.S.

Illustrated with wonderful photographs by the AUTHOR and C. J. KING.

Demy quarto, cloth, gilt, 6s. 3d. *net ; by inland post,* 6s. 9d.

This fascinating book on the Peregrine Falcon—the grandest bird of prey left in England—combines the salient facts of almost innumerable field notes *written at the eyrie itself*. It is a book that should appeal with irresistible force to all true nature lovers. Many striking and unexpected facts were revealed to the author as a result of unwearying patience in a diminutive hut slung from the precipice of a lonely islet. These records are now set forth in a wonderful narrative which discloses the life-history of the Peregrine Falcon from the moment of its hatching to the day it finally leaves the eyrie.

The Times says :—"We commend this faithful and truly scientific inquiry to all lovers of animals and to those who are in quest of a real knowledge of nature."

PRINTED BY
HAZELL, WATSON AND VINEY, LD.,
LONDON AND AYLESBURY.

CPSIA information can be obtained at www.ICGtesting.com
Printed in the USA
LVOW130234051111

253636LV00018B/41/P